4/08

☜ W9-BRP-275

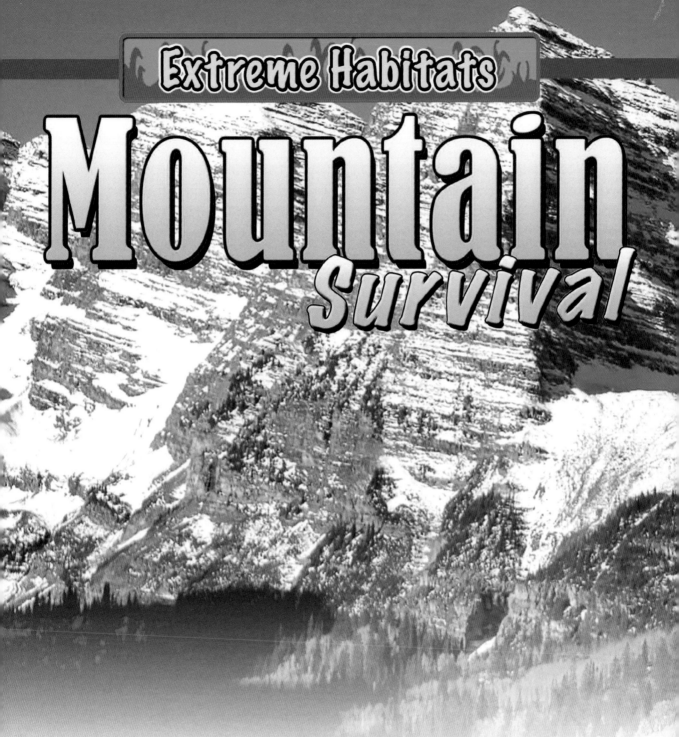

Extreme Habitats

Mountain
Survival

by Susie Hodge

Consultant: Alton Byers, Ph.D., The Mountain Institute

Gareth Stevens
Publishing

Please visit our web site at: www.garethstevens.com
For a free color catalog describing Gareth Stevens Publishing's list
of high-quality books, call 1-800-542-2595 (USA) or 1-800-387-3178 (Canada).

Library of Congress Cataloging-in-Publication Data

Hodge, Susie.
    Mountain survival / Susie Hodge. — North American ed.
      p. cm. — (Extreme habitats)
    Includes index.
    ISBN: 978-0-8368-8246-9 (lib. bdg.)
    1. Mountain ecology—Juvenile literature. I. Title.
  QH541.5.M65H62   2007
  551.43'2—dc22   2007015841

This North American edition first published in 2008 by
Gareth Stevens Publishing
A Weekly Reader® Company
1 Reader's Digest Road
Pleasantville, NY 10570-7000 USA

This U.S. edition copyright © 2008 by Gareth Stevens, Inc.
Original edition copyright © 2007 ticktock Entertainment Ltd.
First published in Great Britain in 2007 by ticktock Media Ltd.,
Unit 2, Orchard Business Centre, North Farm Road,
Tunbridge Wells, Kent, TN2 3XF, United Kingdom

ticktock project editor: Rebecca Clunes
ticktock project designer: Sara Greasley

Gareth Stevens managing editor: Valerie J. Weber
Gareth Stevens editor: Tea Benduhn
Gareth Stevens art direction: Tammy West
Gareth Stevens graphic designer: Dave Kowalski
Gareth Stevens production: Jessica Yanke

Photo credits: (t=top, b=bottom, c=center, l=left, r=right)
Alamy blickwinkel/Alamy 10 – 11c; Bill Crouse 12b; Marcos Delgado/epa/Corbis 17t; Ulrich Doering/Alamy 25cb; Corbis Didrik Johnck/Corbis
9cr; Bryan Knox/Papilio/Corbis 21ct; Craig Lovell/Corbis 24; Luiz Claudio Marigo/naturepl.com 20t; Wally McNamee/Corbis 27ct; Shutterstock
2, 3, 4 – 5 (all), 6-7 (all), 8t, 8 – 9b, 9t, 9cl, 10t, 10b, 11r, 11b, 12t, 13 (all), 14t, 14 – 15, 15cr, 16b, 17tr, 18 – 19 (all), 20b, 21t, 21b, 22t, 23 (all),
25t, 25ct, 25b, 26 (all), 27t, 27cb, 27b, 28t, 28b, 29; Jim Sugar/Getty 16l; Ticktock Media Archive 21cb, 22b, 32; Henrik Trygg/Corbis 15br; Karl
Weatherly/Corbis 15cl. All artwork Ticktock Media Archive except 4 and 17b Cosmographics.

Every effort has been made to trace the copyright holders for the photos used in this book. The publisher apologizes,
in advance, for any unintentional omissions and would be pleased to insert the appropriate acknowledgements in any
subsequent edition of this publication.

Printed in the United States of America

1 2 3 4 5 6 7 8 9 11 10 09 08 07

Contents

Words that appear in the glossary are printed in **boldface**
type the first time they occur in the text.

What Is a Mountain?

Mountains are huge masses of rock with steep *slopes* that are much higher than the land around them. A group of mountains can form a range so huge that it affects the weather across entire continents.

This map shows some of the world's most important mountains and mountain ranges.

Earth's **crust** is made of huge slabs called **plates**, which fit together like a jigsaw puzzle. When plates collide, they can push land upward, producing mountains. It takes millions of years for these strong underground forces to form mountains.

Trees and plants cover mountains' lower slopes. As you go higher above **sea level**, temperatures drop. The tops of many mountains are covered with snow all year. Due to a mountain's height, its **foothills** can have a **tropical** climate, while its peak is icy cold.

The weather can form pointed peaks on mountains. Water enters cracks in the rocks and freezes. Frozen water expands, causing rocks to split and fall away from the mountain.

MOUNTAIN NOTEBOOK

- Mountains influence rainfall. On Big Island in Hawaii, mountains block rainclouds from traveling southwest. The northeastern part of the island gets 10 feet (3 meters) of rain per year, while the southwestern part gets just 30 inches (75 centimeters).

Mountains in Hawaii

- Mountains cover about one-fourth of Earth's surface, and they are found in three-fourths of the world's countries.

MOUNTAIN SURVIVAL TIPS

Hypothermia occurs when your body temperature drops too low. To prevent it, always wear a hat. Most of your body heat is lost through your head.

ax

clips

crampons

Crampons are metal spikes at the bottom of shoes. They fit over climbing boots. They help climbers grip the ice and hard snow.

Journey to the Top of the World

Although mountains are breathtaking to look at, they can be dangerous to climb. If you want to get to the tops of the highest mountains, you must be healthy and have the proper training. It is also important to bring the right equipment.

For some people, climbing mountains is just for fun. For others, like those on **mountain rescue teams**, climbing mountains is part of their job.

There are two main dangers when climbing mountains. You could fall off the side of the mountain or into a **crevasse**, or things, such as rocks and ice, could fall on you.

There are no garbage cans on mountain tops, and nobody will collect your trash for you. Everything you take up, you must bring down.

Safety is essential.
Wear a hard helmet and bring
an ice ax and clips for climbing.

MOUNTAIN SURVIVAL TIPS

Dehydration occurs when your body does not have enough water. Remember to bring water purifying tablets and fuel for your stove. You may not be able to find water on a mountain, but you can melt snow!

A mountain climber needs a large backpack to carry all the equipment!

MOUNTAIN EQUIPMENT

To climb mountains, you must be well equipped. Bring

- Ropes, clamps, and other mountaineering equipment
- An ice ax
- Lots of layers of warm, lightweight clothing
- Sturdy boots
- Helmet, headlight, and goggles
- Several pairs of gloves
- Sunscreen and lip balm
- A two-way radio and satellite phone
- A tent and sleeping bag

Brightly colored tents are easy to see in the snow.

- A small stove, gas-based fuel, and cooking equipment
- Food supplies (high-energy food that cooks quickly)
- A container to collect snow and ice for melting
- Air tanks of bottled **oxygen**

The Highest Place on Earth

Prayer flags fly at a camp on Mount Everest. Local people believe the wind carries their prayers to the gods.

The highest mountain in the world is Mount Everest at 29,037 feet (8,850 m) above sea level. There is one mountain that is actually taller than Everest, but most of it is under water. Only 13,797 feet (4,205 m) of Hawaii's **Mauna Kea** *rise above the sea.*

Mount Everest is in the Himalayas, which are in southern Asia on the border between Nepal and China. Every year, hundreds of people try to climb Everest. Nearly two thousand people have reached the top, but more than two hundred of them have never returned.

Mountain climbing requires more than physical strength. Could you cope with the long, exhausting days, the strong winds, and the freezing cold?

The highest slopes of Everest are almost lifeless. No plants live above about 19,690 feet (6,000 m).

MOUNTAIN SURVIVAL TIPS

Low oxygen levels at the tops of mountains can cause extreme tiredness, headaches, and confusion. If you plan to climb to the top, bring bottled oxygen.

Most expeditions climb the lower slopes of Mount Everest slowly, spending weeks getting used to the low oxygen levels at high **altitudes**. Above 26,250 feet (8,000 m), oxygen levels are so low that people cannot survive for long. The area above this altitude is called the death zone.

People who want to climb Mount Everest get experience by climbing smaller mountains first.

MOUNTAIN NOTEBOOK

- The world's tallest skyscraper, Taipei 101, is 1,670 feet (509 m) tall. Mount Everest is more than seventeen times higher than that.

- Mount Everest is growing by about 0.2 inch (about 5 millimeters) each year!

Above 26,250 feet (8,000 m), climbers wear oxygen masks all the time, even while relaxing.

- Only people in groups are allowed to climb Mount Everest. No one goes alone. The smallest number of people in a team is seven. They pay thousands of dollars for a permit to climb.

The Longest Ranges

Farmers high up in the Andes raise llamas for their wool.

Some mountains are single peaks, but most occur in ranges. Mountain ranges can stretch long distances. The world's longest mountain range is the Mid-Atlantic Ridge, which runs for nearly 9,940 miles (16,000 kilometers) beneath the Atlantic Ocean.

On land, the longest mountain chain is the Andes, which stretches across seven South American countries. It is 4,500 miles (7,240 km) long and about 150 miles (240 km) wide. The average height of the Andes is about 12,000 feet (3,660 m).

The South American condor lives in the Andes. Its outstretched wings can measure up to 10 feet (3 m) across.

Machu Picchu in Peru is the site of an ancient Incan village. It is 7,970 feet (2,430 m) high in the Andes, and it is visited by thousands of tourists every year.

The Andes run from north of the warm **equator** to the southern tip of South America. Their tallest mountain is Aconcagua in Argentina, which is 22,835 feet (6,960 m) high. Most of the highest mountains in the Andes are **volcanoes**. One of the highest volcanoes in the world is Cotopaxi in Ecuador. It is 19,348 feet (5,897 m) tall.

The longest mountain chain in North America is the Rocky Mountains, also called the Rockies. They stretch 2,000 miles (3,220 km) down the western edge of Canada and the United States.

Maroon Bells in Colorado are just one of the many hundreds of mountains that form the Rockies.

MOUNTAIN NOTEBOOK

- Many minerals can be found in the Andes. Some of them include gold, silver, tin, copper, platinum, lead, and zinc.

Gold can be found throughout the Andes.

- The Andes Mountains are so high that they can block winds and rain clouds. Some mountains' eastern slopes are covered in rain forests while the western slopes are dry, desert land.

MOUNTAIN SURVIVAL TIPS

Extreme cold can damage your skin and cause frostbite. In some cases of frostbite, your skin can become black and swollen. Protect your ears, nose, fingers, toes, and cheeks.

The Worst Weather

A sudden snowstorm forms in the Sierra Nevada mountain range in California.

The higher you climb up a mountain, the harder the winds blow, making you feel even colder. Gales and blizzards make travel difficult and dangerous. Mountain climbers watch the weather carefully. They must change their plans if the conditions become too dangerous.

Weather on mountains often changes suddenly. Within minutes, a bright sunny day can change to freezing cold rain. Blizzards are particularly dangerous because the driving snow makes it hard for mountain climbers to see where they are going.

Some times of the year are better for climbing than others. Mount Everest, for example, has just two **weather windows**. These periods last four to five days during the spring. During this time, the weather is less likely to be dangerous for climbers.

Even in bright sunshine, the temperature on Mount Everest is well below freezing. Climbers cover up as much as possible.

Buildings on Mount Rainier in Washington state must be able to withstand heavy snowfalls.

Mount McKinley in Alaska is one of the coldest mountains on Earth. The average temperature in January is −6 °Fahrenheit (−21 °Celsius). This mountain has the highest peak in North America. It is dangerous to climb, too. Nearly one hundred people have died trying to get to the top.

MOUNTAIN NOTEBOOK

- Wind rushes up mountains during the day and down them during the night.

- Lightning tends to strike the highest point in an area, so it can be especially dangerous on mountains during a storm.

Lightning strikes mountains.

- More mountain climbers die from being battered by blizzards than by falling.

MOUNTAIN SURVIVAL TIPS

Bright sunlight reflects from the snow and ice into your eyes. Wear goggles to avoid snow blindness, which causes blurry vision and pain.

Mount McKinley offers breathtaking views.

The Most Dangerous to Climb

The Himalayan mountain range has some of the highest mountains in the world.

K2 in the Himalayas is 28,253 feet (8,611 m) tall. It is the second highest mountain in the world and one of the most difficult to climb. Although it is not as tall as Mount Everest, the climbing conditions on K2 are often more challenging.

Above 19,690 feet (6,000 m), thick snow and ice blankets K2. This mountain has none of the weather windows that Mount Everest has. It is almost impossible to climb K2 without getting caught in life-threatening weather.

On K2, mountain climbers rope themselves to each other for safety.

If you get buried in snow from an avalanche, your rescuers will need to act fast. The weight of the snow will make it hard for you to breathe, which is more likely to kill you than the cold.

K2 is also dangerous because its slopes are extremely steep. **Avalanches** are common on these slopes, and climbers need special mountaineering equipment for climbing.

Fewer than 250 people have climbed to the top of K2. Of those climbers, 10 percent have died on their way back down.

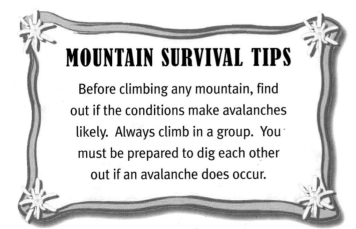

MOUNTAIN SURVIVAL TIPS

Before climbing any mountain, find out if the conditions make avalanches likely. Always climb in a group. You must be prepared to dig each other out if an avalanche does occur.

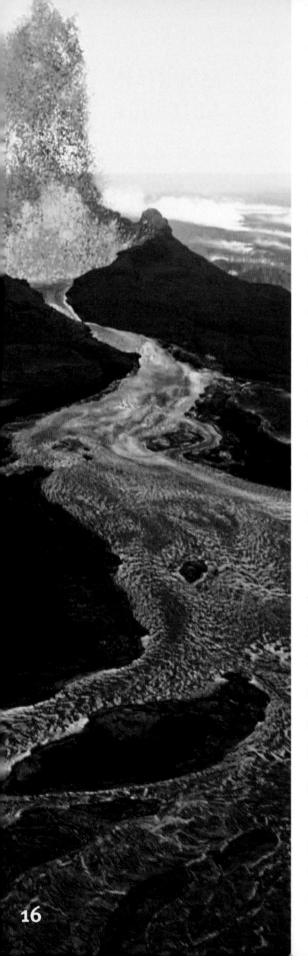

Deadly Mountains

Do you think climbing a mountain is dangerous? There are lots of other dangers, too! Look out for volcanoes, flash floods, and landslides. People can be swept away, burned, drowned, or buried under deep, choking mud.

Openings in Earth's crust, volcanoes are the deadliest mountains of all. An erupting volcano can send fiery clouds of hot ash, gas, and red-hot liquid rock into the sky. The liquid rock, called lava, flows down the mountain at temperatures up to 1,830 °F (1,000 °C).

International scientists regularly keep a close watch over sixteen particular volcanoes. Two of the volcanoes are Mount Rainier in Washington State and Mount Etna in Italy. These volcanoes are dangerous because they have a high risk of erupting. Many people live near them, however, because volcanic soil is good for growing grass for animals and crops.

Some volcanoes erupt from deep below the sea and form islands. Over time, as these volcanoes continue to erupt, the islands grow.

A mud landslide has run down the slopes of a mountain in Guatemala and buried the village at the bottom.

Landslides can be particularly damaging to mountains without forests on their lower slopes. Without a forest, with its strong network of roots and ability to soak up rainfall, soil is washed away in huge mud rivers that destroy everything in their paths.

The orange triangles on the map show active volcanoes around the Pacific Ocean. This area is known as the Ring of Fire. Volcanoes usually occur near plate boundaries, which are also marked in orange on the map.

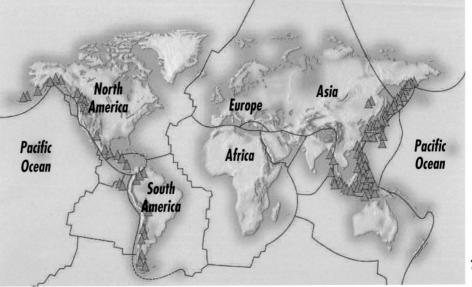

17

Majestic Mountains

Three huge pillars of rock, the Three Sisters stand in the Blue Mountains in Australia.

Majestic and awesome, high peaks often spark amazement in people who see them. This sense of wonder is why so many people want to climb tall mountains, despite the dangers.

Some mountains are considered **sacred**. Mount Fuji in Japan is one such mountain. More than 200,000 people climb to the top each year to pray. Most people climb Mount Fuji in two days, staying overnight in special mountain huts.

Most countries are proud of their mountains and make the surrounding areas into national parks. The **Blue Mountains** in Australia are a national park. Their name comes from the blue haze that is created by oil evaporating from nearby eucalyptus trees.

Mount Fuji is Japan's tallest mountain at 12,389 feet (3,776 m). It is famous for its beautiful shape.

MOUNTAIN NOTEBOOK

- Table Mountain in South Africa was named for its peak, which is as flat as a tabletop. The top is often covered in clouds, which people call "the tablecloth."

Table Mountain, South Africa

- **Mount Kilimanjaro** in Tanzania is the highest mountain in Africa. It is also the world's highest mountain that is not part of a mountain range.

MOUNTAIN SURVIVAL TIPS

IODINE TABLETS

Mountain streams and melted snow can contain germs, so purify your water before you drink it. Add an iodine tablet to water and wait thirty minutes for the water to be **disinfected**.

FACT FILE:

The puya, in the Andes, lives for up to 150 years.
It has the tallest flower of any plant.

Plant Survivors

Plants cannot live without water and minerals. They cannot move around to find what they need, nor can they run from danger. It is difficult for plants to survive in icy temperatures and biting winds, so mountain plants have adapted to extreme conditions.

- The two biggest problems mountain plants face are low temperatures and the lack of water.

- Some plants keep warm with a furry or hairy covering on their leaves and stems. The puya of the Andes protects its giant flower spike with a prickly covering.

The different altitudes at which certain types of plants can live on mountains

ALTITUDE	PLANTS
3,281 FEET (1,000 M)	BROAD LEAFED TREES
6,562 FEET (2,000 M)	CONIFER TREES
9,843 FEET (3,000 M)	SHRUBS
11,483 FEET (3,500 M)	ALPINE FLOWERS
13,124 FEET (4,000 M)	LICHEN

The giant groundsel plant in Africa uses its dead leaves to protect its stem from the cold.

Mountain Plants

- **Edelweisses**
  - In the European **Alps,** tiny edelweiss plants grow in cracks in rocks.
  - Their waxy leaves hold in water, and hairy stems and leaves keep the plants warm.

- **Alpine snowbells**
  - The alpine snowbell pushes its new shoots through the snow each spring. This action gives off enough heat to melt the ice!
  - Its petals vary from blue to purple depending on the habitat.

- **Diapensias**
  - Several mountain plants, such as diapensia, remain small and huddle together in low mounds of tightly packed leaves.
  - Staying close to the ground protects the plants from freezing winds.

Edelweiss

Alpine snowbell

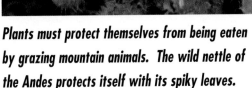

Diapensia

- The hair that covers some plants protects them from the Sun's damaging **ultraviolet** rays. These rays are stronger at high altitudes than anywhere else.

- Some plants have waxy leaves to reduce water loss. Some have absorbent leaves or roots that take in whatever water they can find in high altitudes.

- Some plants have special sap to prevent their cells from freezing solid.

Plants must protect themselves from being eaten by grazing mountain animals. The wild nettle of the Andes protects itself with its spiky leaves.

FACT FILE:

Animal Survivors

*You might think that no animal could cope with the awful weather and steep and slippery slopes of mountains, but several do. Many animals have special **adaptations** for living in mountains, such as warm, thick fur coats.*

According to some estimates, more than thirty thousand mountain lions live in the Rocky Mountains.

● Mountain animals are usually agile and sure-footed. Most can run along steep slopes with ease.

● The mountain goat lives only in North America. It is often found at altitudes as high as 9,840 feet (3,000 m).

MOUNTAIN GOAT ADAPTATIONS

Short body so goat can turn around on narrow ledges

White coat to blend in with the snow

Two layers of hair — a thick undercoat and longer hair on top

Hooves with sharp edges to push into cracks in the rocks

Hollow hooves that stick to rocks like suction cups

Mountain Survivors

- **Mountain gorillas**
  - Mountain gorillas live on high slopes in central Africa.
  - Their fur is longer than other gorillas to protect them from the cold.
  - Fewer than 700 mountain gorillas are living today.

Mountain gorilla

- **Bighorn sheep**
  - These sheep live in the Rocky Mountains. They have good eyesight and hearing to alert them to danger.
  - They eat large amounts of grass and then go to narrow ledges to digest it. While they are digesting their food, they are safe from predators.

Bighorn sheep

  - **Guanacos**
    - Guanacos are part of the camel family, but they do not have humps. They have thick coats of long wool for warmth.
      - They are expert browsers, finding plenty of food in the scrubby grasslands of the Andes.

Guanaco

- Food is scarce, so only a few predators can survive on any mountain. Predators include snow leopards in the Himalayas, mountain lions in parts of the Rocky Mountains, and timber wolves and lynxes on the mountains of Alaska.

  - Only powerful birds can withstand strong mountain winds. These birds include eagles, falcons, and Andean condors. They feed on small mammals.

The bald eagle lives on mountains throughout North America.

FACT FILE:

Mountain People

People who live near sea level often feel dizzy or short of breath if they climb above 9,840 feet (3,000 m). Many people, however, live comfortably in towns along mountain ranges. Wenzhuan in the Himalayas, for example, is 16,730 feet (5,100 m) above sea level.

About 45 percent of the people in Bolivia live at altitudes above 9,840 feet (3,000 m).

- The Quechua Indians live high up in the Andes. They have extra **blood vessels** in their feet to keep them warm.

- To get enough oxygen to their blood, the Quechua Indians have bigger hearts and lungs than most people.

Some of the highest towns in different countries around the world

TOWN	COUNTRY	CONTINENT	ALTITUDE
WENZHUAN	TIBET	ASIA	16,733 feet (5,100 m)
LA RICONADA	PERU	SOUTH AMERICA	16,733 feet (5,100 m)
GAITE	INDIA	ASIA	14,436 feet (4,400 m)
DOLPA	NEPAL	ASIA	14,305 feet (4,360 m)
EL ALTO	BOLIVIA	SOUTH AMERICA	13,452 feet (4,100 m)
APARTADEROS	VENEZUELA	SOUTH AMERICA	11,500 feet (3,505 m)
LEADVILLE	UNITED STATES	NORTH AMERICA	10,434 feet (3,180 m)
QUITO	ECUADOR	SOUTH AMERICA	9,351 feet (2,850 m)
KURUSH	RUSSIA	ASIA	8,137 feet (2,480 m)
EL SERRAT	ANDORRA	EUROPE	7,769 feet (2,368 m)

Around the World

- **Bolivia, South America**
  - The Aymara people of the Andes Mountains live around Lake Titicaca, the highest lake in South America.
  - To catch fish in the lake, they use reeds to make rafts and small rowboats.

Fishing boat on Lake Titicaca

- **Nepal, Asia**
  - Farmers in some parts of Nepal cut giant steps, called terraces, into the hillside. They build walls on the terraces to hold in soil and water.
  - Farmers grow potatoes, rice, wheat, barley, and apricots on terraced fields.

Sherpa farm

- **Tanzania, Africa**
  - People of the Chagga tribe live on the southern and eastern slopes of Mount Kilimanjaro and Mount Meru.
  - Coffee and bananas are the main crops in these mountains.

A Chagga woman carries bananas

- Across parts of northern China, millions of people make their homes in mountain caves called *yaodongs*. Yaodong means "arched tunnel" in Chinese. The mountain **insulates** the caves, keeping them warm in winter and cool in summer.

- Today, some **Sherpa** people make their living guiding tourists up the high mountains of the Himalayas.

The Sherpa people use yaks for plowing their farmland.

FACT FILE:

Many Uses of Mountains

The high slopes of most mountains in the world have been left in their natural state. Many people visit them for sports or recreation. Others use mountains for growing crops. Still other people find medicinal plants high up in the wild.

Skiing is a very popular sport. About 60 million tourists visited the European Alps in 2006.

*The coffee grown in the **Blue Mountains** in Jamaica is considered to be some of the best in the world.*

- Mountain **tourism** has grown. People visit mountains to try out sports, breathe the clear air, or enjoy spectacular views.

- Skiing is a traditional mountain sport. Most mountain sports feature speed and danger, and they require specialized equipment.

- Coffee plants grow best in tropical mountains. High-quality coffee comes from bushes that grow at altitudes above 3,280 feet (1,000 m) although not in areas that receive frost.

- Plants that can be used to make medicines are found on many mountains of the world, such as the Himalayas and the Alps.

New Mountain Sports

- **Snowboarding**
  - This sport is a cross between skateboarding and skiing.
  - The goal of downhill snowboarding is to get to the bottom of the mountain as quickly as possible.
  - Stunts and jumps are important in freestyle snowboarding.

Snowboarding

- **Bobsledding**
  - Sleds run down an icy track with many bends in it.
  - Teams compete to see which one can go the fastest.

Bobsledding

- **Mountain biking**
  - Riders must be able to pedal their bikes up steep hills and control them down sheer slopes.
  - Mountain bikes have lots of gears and thick tires with bumpy treads to grip the surface of the rocky ground.

Mountain biking

- Almost all medicinal mountain plants are collected from the wild. They are not farmed like other crops.

Some of these mountain plants are used in traditional medicines.

PLANT	FOUND IN	HELPS TREAT
BARBERRY	HIMALAYAS	EYE DISEASES
GENTIANS	ANDES	LIVER PROBLEMS
HIMALAYAN YEW	HIMALAYAS	CANCER
PERUVIAN BARK	ANDES	MALARIA
SNOW LOTUS	HIMALAYAS	RHEUMATISM
SWERTIA	HIMALAYAS	HEART PROBLEMS

The bark of the barberry plant is used to treat sore eyes and fevers.

FACT FILE:

Mountains in Danger

Mountain habitats are more fragile than they look. Some problems are caused by the people who live in them, such as people who cut down trees for firewood. Other damage is caused by companies that mine them or by tourists who visit the mountains.

Only 500 people per day are allowed to walk the Inca Trail in Peru. This limit is set to protect the vulnerable mountain path.

- Some people cut down forests for firewood or lumber. With fewer trees, rain washes away the soil. The soil clogs rivers, which can cause a shortage of water farther down the mountain.

- Climbers have dumped about 66 tons (60 tonnes) of garbage on Mount Everest, including cans, plastic containers, glass, clothes, and tents.

- On several mountains, including Mount Everest, if you are caught dropping litter, you could pay a large fine.

This mountain in Nepal has been nicknamed Fishtail because its top looks like a fish's tail. It is a sacred mountain, and climbers are not allowed up it.

Types of Mountains

People can have a big effect on the environment of mountain slopes, but it is hard to change the mountain itself. Mountains are usually formed over thousands of years, and people are not able to influence this process.

- **Fold mountains**
  - Movement of Earth's plates can cause layers of rocks to push against each other.
  - The rocks crumple and bulge. Mountains are pushed up, and valleys are squeezed down.
  - Most of the mountains in the Alps are fold mountains.

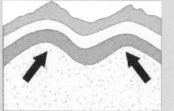

Fold mountain

- **Fault mountains**
  - The surface of the Earth sometimes cracks along a **fault**.
  - Layers of rock on one side of the crack can be pushed up to form a mountain.

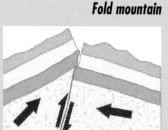

Fault mountain

- **Volcanic mountains**
  - When a volcano erupts, it pushes out lava.
  - The lava hardens and cools, sometimes forming a mountain.
  - Mount Fuji and Mount Vesuvius are examples of volcanic mountains.

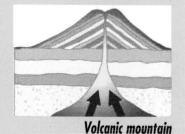

Volcanic mountain

- Thankfully, most people who visit mountains treat the unique environment with respect. They follow the saying "take only pictures, leave only footprints."

People are beginning to realize the dangers of cutting down mountain forests, and they are now planting new trees.

Glossary

adaptations — changes made by plants, animals, and people to fit their environments

Alps — a mountain range in Europe

altitudes — the heights above a certain point, such as sea level

avalanches — sliding masses of snow and ice that can move at speeds of more than 1 mile (2 km) per minute

blood vessels — tubes that carry blood around the body

Blue Mountains — 1. A group of cliffs in southern Australia that are about 3,281 feet (1,000 m) high 2. A mountainous region of Jamaica

crevasse — a deep crack in the ground

crust — the outer layer of Earth

dehydration — the condition of not having enough water in the body

disinfected — cleansed or freed from harmful germs

equator — an imaginary line around the middle of Earth

fault — a crack in Earth's crust, often where plates meet

flash floods — sudden rushes of water after heavy rains

foothills — low hills at the bottoms of mountains

hypothermia — the condition of the body's temperature dropping dangerously low. It can cause a person to be unable to move properly or think clearly.

insulates — protects something from heat or cold by covering it

K2 — the world's second highest mountain, which lies on the borders of Pakistan and China in the Himalayas

landslides — rapid movements of earth and rocks down a mountain

Mauna Kea — the tallest mountain in the world, as measured from its base to its top. It is 33,476 feet (10,203 m) tall, but 19,679 feet (5,998 m) of it are under water.

mountain rescue teams — groups of people who look for climbers and hikers who have become lost

Mount Kilimanjaro — located in Tanzania, this mountain is 19,341 feet (5,895 m) tall

oxygen — a gas in Earth's atmosphere that animals need to live

plates — huge slabs that form Earth's crust. Continents and oceans rest upon these plates which are moving slowly all the time.

sacred — describes something, such as a person, place, or object, that a group of people considers to be holy

sea level — the height of the sea's surface when it is midway between high and low tide. It is used as a starting point for measuring the height of mountains or other objects.

Sherpa — a member of a Tibetan people who are from the eastern part of Nepal

slopes — the sides of mountains

tropical — relating to the areas of the world near the equator where the weather is often hot and humid

tourism — an industry that is based on people visiting places of interest

ultraviolet — invisible rays given off by the Sun that can cause damage to plants, animals, and people

volcanoes — mountains formed by lava that is forced up through an opening in the earth. Volcanoes often have a hollow top.

weather windows — periods of good weather in between periods of storms

For Further Information

Books

Mountains. Biomes (series). Erinn Banting (Weigl Publishing)

Mountains. Library of Landforms (series). Isaac Nadeau (PowerKids Press)

Rocky Mountains. Our Wild World (series). Wayne Lynch (Northword Press)

Web Sites

Denali for Kids
pbskids.org/nova/denali
Click on the links to find out about survival skills, meals, and more.

Volcano! Mountain of Fire.
www.nationalgeographic.com/ngkids/0312/main.html
Click "enter" to find out more about volcanoes from National Geographic Kids.

Publisher's note to educators and parents: Our editors have carefully reviewed these Web sites to ensure that they are suitable for children. Many Web sites change frequently, however, and we cannot guarantee that a site's future contents will continue to meet our high standards of quality and educational value. Be advised that children should be closely supervised whenever they access the Internet.

Index